A RANCHER'S GUIDE TO LIFE

THE QUOTATIONS IN THIS BOOK COME FROM A MIXTURE OF LORE AND EXPERIENCE.

A RANCHER'S GUIDE TO LIFE

TEXAS BIX BENDER

GIBBS SMITH
TO ENRICH AND INSPIRE HUMANKIND

Never play leapfrog
with a bull.

LIGHTNING DOES THE WORK,

THUNDER TAKES THE CREDIT.

IF YOU'RE APPROACHING LAND'S END, YOU NEED A CATTLE-LOG.

FOR EVERY MILE
OF BAD ROAD
YOU TRAVEL,
THERE'RE TWO
MILES OF DITCH
YOU'RE STAYIN'
OUT OF.

Overweight cows should rest against
objects in a standing position;

this will make them lean.

YOU CAN FORCE A HERD TO FOLLOW
A PATH OF ACTION, BUT YOU CAN'T
FORCE THEM TO UNDERSTAND IT.

YOU CAN ALWAYS TELL A BULL, BUT YOU CAN'T TELL HIM MUCH.

TO A COW, EVERY DAY IS JUST AN UDDER DAY.

SET YOUR PACE BY THE DISTANCE YOU'VE GOTTA GO.

Conform and

be dull.

When you find yourself in over your
head, don't open your mouth.

SWIM!

Sometimes the only way to grab a bull by the horns

is to slap on the hobbles.

One man's
sacred cow
is another's
Big Mac.

PULLIN'
SOMETHIN' UP BY
ITS ROOTS WON'T
HELP IT GROW.

Let us honor if we can the
vertical cow, though we value
none but the slaughtered one.
—W.H. Aberdeen

CHANGE THE ENVIRONMENT, DON'T TRY TO CHANGE THE COW.

—Buckminster Bull

There is nothing like lying on your belly in soft, cool mud.

"Weighs a ton, eyes of dun, Could she, could she, could she moo,

Has anybody seen my cow?"

THERE ARE HUNDREDS OF USES
FOR COWHIDE.
BUT THE MOST IMPORTANT IS
TO HOLD THE COW TOGETHER.

EVERYBODY'S A RIDER ON A GENTLE HORSE.

IF YOU CROSS A
BRIDGE BEFORE
YOU GET TO IT,
YOU PAY THE
TOLL TWICE.

DON'T HAVE A COW UNLESS YOU ARE A COW.

**When things
go wrong,**

**don't go
with them.**

You can
lead a cow
to fodder,
but you
can't make
her think.

NEVER CUT WHAT
YOU CAN UNTIE.

Getting off the
bull is harder
than getting on.

A GOOD FRIEND MAKES EVERY MILE YOU TRAVEL TOGETHER

A LITTLE SHORTER.

WHEN IN DOUBT, LET YOUR HORSE DO THE THINKIN'.

It's better to cross the muddy
ground to the hay than to
stand and long to be there.

A little music in the
barn puts a cow
in the mooood.

IF YOU PARLEY WITH THE WRONG SIDE,

YOU'LL NEVER GET ON THE RIGHT SIDE.

FEAST AND YOU
ALWAYS HAVE
COMPANY.

★★★

FAST AND YOU
FAST ALONE.

If faced with a choice between an open
gate and a bale of hay, take the hay.

If you're hell-bent
for leather, you'll get
where you're goin'.

A HERD IS THE RESULT OF LOVE IN BLOOM.

SHALLOW STREAMS AND SHALLOW MINDS FREEZE FIRST.

Frustration is
having a stump
tail in fly season.

IF YOU WANT TO WORK
UP TO BEIN' A GOOD
RIDER, YOU'VE GOT SOME
MUD TO EAT.

It takes more
than a pat on
the back to cure
saddle sores.

KEEP YOUR FACE TO THE SUN AND THE SHADOWS WILL FALL BEHIND YOU.

I once went all day without food
and all night without sleep to
enable me to think. It was a waste
of time. Cows can't think.
—Tao of Moo

THE BRIDGES YOU CROSS BEFORE
YOU COME TO THEM ARE USUALLY
OVER RIVERS THAT AREN'T THERE.

AUTOMOBILES SHOULD BE SHOT WHEN THEY BREAK DOWN.

Two heads are not
better than one,

but two
stomachs are.

WHAT IS
NATURAL AND
WHAT IS RIGHT
MAKE PRETTY
GOOD GROUND
TO STAND ON.

When the herd turns on you and you're forced to run for it, try to look like you're leading the charge.

ALL COWS LOOK ALIKE,
BUT THEIR FACES ARE
DIFFERENT SO YOU CAN
TELL THEM APART.

Pint-size ponies like to snort and stomp just a much as big ones.

IF TOMBSTONES TOLD
THE TRUTH, HELL
WOULD HAVE GONE OUT
OF BUSINESS LONG AGO.

LIFE IS LIKE A COW PASTURE.

It's very hard to get through it without stepping in some muck.

When you have a
cud to chew, how
can you know
about death?

COWS HAVE THEIR FAULTS,

BUT EATING MEAT ISN'T
ONE OF THEM.

IF YOU CAN KEEP YOUR HEAD WHILE ALL ABOUT YOU ARE LOSING THEIRS,

YOU OBVIOUSLY DON'T UNDERSTAND THE SITUATION.

WHEN YOU'RE RUNNIN' FROM SOMETHIN', IT'S STILL GOOD TO KNOW WHERE YOU'RE GOIN'.

No Flies Can
Enter a
Closed Mouth.

BETTER FROM THE
HORSE'S MOUTH THAN
A HORSE'S BEHIND.

MOO LOW,
MOO SLOW,
AND DON'T MOO
TOO MUCH.
    —DUKE LONGHORN

IT'S NOT TRUE
THAT LIFE IS
JUST ONE DARN
THING AFTER
ANOTHER.

IT'S THE SAME
DARN THING
OVER AND OVER.

Weight and brands are hard to hide.

WITH TIME AND PATIENCE, ALL THE APPLES CAN BE EATEN.

When you tie on the feed bag, be
content with a genteel sufficiency.

Any more than that is a vulgar plenty.

THE MOST SUCCESSFUL LIAR IS THE ONE WHO DOESN'T DO IT TOO OFTEN.

THERE ARE MORE HORSES' PATOOTS THAN HORSES.

IT'S BETTER TO BE IN THE BACK OF THE HERD AND BE DISCOVERED, THAN TO BE IN FRONT AND BE FOUND OUT.

THE BIGGER THE SPUR, THE BIGGER THE PRICK.

When you have to hobble a cow,

a little grain softens the misery.

WHEN THE BULL
IS LOOSE . . .

NO SUDDEN MOVES.

ON A CLEAR DAY
YOU CAN RIDE
FOREVER.

Things have a way of workin'
out if you can just keep your
head out of your behind.

GOOD FENCES MAKE BULLS GOOD NEIGHBORS.

It is not possible to run from something you are tied to.

**ABOUT HALF
A MIND TO DO
SOMETHING
USUALLY GETS
IT ABOUT
HALF DONE.**

YOU DON'T HAVE TO
SEE THE LIGHT
TO FEEL THE HEAT.

THERE'S NOTHING LIKE A STABLE ENVIRONMENT TO MAKE A COW CONTENTED.

Start off as you

mean to go.

COMPLAINING HAS ABOUT AS MUCH EFFECT AS THE BARKING OF A FARAWAY DOG.

Being stubborn is
the only way to
stand out in a herd.

A HORSE IS STILL A HORSE
WITHOUT A RIDER,

BUT A RIDER WITHOUT A
HORSE IS AFOOT.

A CHANGE OF PASTURE CAN LEAD TO A FATTER CALF.

If you want a horse to know
you, breathe up its nose the
first time you meet.

**DROWNIN'
YOUR SORROWS
SELDOM WORKS,**

**AS MOST OF 'EM
CAN SWIM.**

If you can't be
the bell cow,
fall in behind;
★ ★ ★
you'll still get there.

FOR THOUSANDS OF YEARS
COYOTES HAVE HOWLED
AT THE MOON . . .

STILL NO ANSWER.

IF YOU NEVER CLIMB A HILL,

you will never know it is different from a plain.

Nobody ever
asks how
many miles a
horse gets to a
bale of hay.

★ ★ ★

THERE IS ART EVEN IN THE CLEANING OF A STABLE.

We think as a herd. We succumb
to madness as a herd.

WE COME TO
OUR SENSES AS
INDIVIDUALS.

MANY ARE CALLED BUT FEW GET UP.

THE SADDLE DON'T MAKE THE HORSE.

EVERY JACKASS THINKS HE'S GOT HORSE SENSE.

When you get
up to look, you
lose your place.

THE WORLD DOESN'T MIND
A CLEVER COW, AS LONG
AS THE COW IS THE ONLY
ONE WHO KNOWS.

BETTER TO HAVE A GOOD HOLD

THAN A GOOD PLACE TO FALL.

BULLS SELDOM MAKE PASSES AT HEIFERS WITH GASES.

**Let the wind
do your sighing
and the clouds
cry your tears.**

IF YOU STICK YOUR NOSE INTO TROUBLE, YOUR FEET ARE BOUND TO FOLLOW.

MOOING IS EASY WHEN YOU DON'T KNOW HOW.

THERE ARE MANY CONTENTED COWS,

BUT WHO HAS HEARD OF A CONTENTED RANCHER?

To know the total of the herd, count
the hooves and divide by four.

WHAT IS TIME TO A RANCH ANIMAL?

IT'S IMPORTANT TO UNDERSTAND TIME. THE ONLY INSTRUMENT THAT TELLS TIME ACCURATELY IS THE STOMACH. WHEN WE GET HUNGRY, IT'S TIME TO EAT. BEYOND THAT, TIME MAKES LITTLE DIFFERENCE.

A GENTLE HORSE IS SOON CURRIED.

It ain't over till
the fat cow sings.

CRAP NOT ONLY HAPPENS,
IT MAKES THINGS GROW.

If anyone asks what a herd is,

★ ★ ★

the answer, for all practical purposes,
is whatever the herd thinks it is.

IF YOU CAN'T SEE THE BOTTOM, DON'T GO IN.

YOU MISS A LOT WHEN YOU TRAVEL AT A GALLOP.

THE BEST WAY OUT IS
USUALLY
TO GO ON THROUGH.

THE NICE THING ABOUT EATING GRASS IS THAT THERE ARE NO BONES IN IT.

WORRYING IS LIKE STANDING
IN A MUD HOLE:

IT GIVES YOU SOMETHING
TO DO, BUT IT DOESN'T
GET YOU ANYWHERE.

NOT EVEN A COW
WANTS TO STAY BAREFOOT
AND PREGNANT.

A good bowel
is worth more
than any amount
of brains.

YOU CAN'T INSULT ARROGANCE.

Every horse looks
tall in a short herd.

A RIVER CAN'T BE MEASURED WITH A TASTE.

You have to control yourself before
you can control your horse.

COLD HANDS

★ ★ ★

WARM MILK

★ ★ ★

AGITATED COW.

MISTAKES ARE LESSONS TO BE LEARNED

BEFORE THE FLOWERS OF FRIENDSHIP FADE, EAT THEM.

— GERTRUDE HOLSTEIN

Passing judgment
is not a good
course to pass.

A contented belly makes
for a happy heart.

NOT MAKIN' A CHOICE
IS MAKIN' A CHOICE.

LOVE NEEDS CONSTANT NOURISHMENT.

Waitin' is easy if
your foot's not the
one needin' a shoe.

YOU CAN'T PUT A MIRROR
ON THE TABLE AND EAT
ON YOUR GOOD LOOKS.

WHAT YOU CAN'T JUMP, YOU GOTTA GO AROUND.

WHEN THE HORSE IS SPENT, A STRONGER WHIP WON'T REFRESH HIM.

Horses can't speak
English, but they do
speak fluent horse.

GET ALL THE FOOLS ON
YOUR SIDE AND YOU CAN
LEAD THE HERD.

WHEN SHADE IS SPARSE, IT MUST BE SHARED.

HAVE CONFIDENCE
IN YOUR SEAT

AND YOU WILL
NOT LOSE IT.

The diet is a little
monotonous,

★ ★ ★

but the atmosphere
is terrific.

Where have all the flowers gone?
Cows ate them every one.
When will they ever learn?
When will they ever learn?

THE THOUSAND-MILE
TRAIL DRIVE ENDS WITH
THE LAST STEP.

Don't eat
anything
that has a
face on it.

I AM MYSELF AND ALL THAT IS
AROUND ME, BUT IF I DO NOT EAT
IT, IT SHALL NOT BE ME.

—THE TAO OF MOO

There may come a day when the cow
and the lion will lie down together—
but the cow won't get much sleep.

IF LIFE IS GOIN'
BY TOO FAST,
TRY SLOWIN'
DOWN A BIT ON
THE TURNS.

IF YOU'RE BEING CHASED BY A BULL
WHILE YOU'RE MILKING THE COW,
GO AHEAD AND MILK THE COW;
YOU CAN ALWAYS SHOOT THE BULL.

EVERY TAIL
HAS AN END.

IF YOU WANT TO SWIM,

★ ★ ★

YOU'VE GOTTA GO WHERE THE WATER IS DEEP.

The farther you run away,

the farther it is back.

TO ERR IS HUMAN

THEREFORE, COWS CAN DO NO WRONG.

An unsaddled pony will often show no
vice at all, but when ridden and fed
he may display all manner of sin.

THE BEST INDICATION OF WHAT WOULD HAVE HAPPENED IS WHAT DID HAPPEN.

There's nothin' like a good long walk,

especially if it's taken by somebody
you'd like to get rid of.

YOU HAVE TO LOVE A WOMAN TO KNOW HER. EVEN THEN, THERE'S A LOT OF GUESSWORK INVOLVED.

Two's company, three's a herd.

Nothing is more than half as good as it would be if it was twice as good as it is. On the other hand, everything is twice as good as it would be, if it were only half as good as it is.

A YOUNG PONY IS
QUICK TO PICK UP
AN OLD HORSE'S
BAD HABITS.

KNOW YOUR LIMITS OR
YOU'LL FIND YOURSELF
ALL HOBBLED UP WITH
EVERYWHERE TO GO.

If it's too much to
love your enemy,
then compromise

★ ★ ★

and just forget
the knothead.

If you have to
run for it, do
so before you
have to.

EVEN THE POOREST COW
HAS A LEATHER COAT.

PEOPLE SHOULDN'T GO AROUND

ACTIN' LIKE ANY PART OF A HORSE.

It does no good
to sell your horse
to buy a saddle.

TWO'S A COINCIDENCE,

THREE'S AN OUTBREAK.

LIFE IS NOW, AND THEN.

TOMORROW IS NEVER.

Let the cow into paradise

and leave the bull behind.

THE NUMBER OF TRAFFIC
ACCIDENTS THAT HAPPEN EVERY
YEAR PRETTY MUCH PROVES THAT
MOST OF THE HORSE SENSE IN THE
HORSE-AND-BUGGY DAYS BELONGED
TO THE HORSE.

IT'S BETTER TO REMOVE A BULL'S HORNS ALL AT ONCE THAN AN INCH AT A TIME.

YOU CAN LEAD A FOOL
TO TALK, BUT YOU CAN'T
MAKE HIM THINK.

If you're following a cow,
you should know
that in all likelihood,
it too is following a cow.

THE GOBBLER
DOESN'T SPREAD
HIS TAIL
FEATHERS WHEN
HIS HEAD'S ON
THE BLOCK.

If you wait 'til the cows come home, the hills are alive with the sound of mooosic.

Swallow what you're
chewin' before you
take the next bite.

A COW CHIP IS A PICNIC TO A FLY.

A pony that shies
and rears is
unsafe in traffic.

A LOT OF MUD HOLES ARE DEEPER THAN THEY LOOK.

A HERD OF A THOUSAND COWS
BEGINS WITH A SINGLE BULL.

IF YOU CAN'T FIGHT THEM,

AND THEY WON'T LET YOU JOIN THEM,

FIND ANOTHER PASTURE.

An old horse for a
long hard road,

a young pony for
a quick ride.

YOU CAN'T JUDGE A HORSE
BY ITS COLOR.

A BAD HORSE IS OFTEN A
GOOD COLOR.

IF YOU HAVE TO CLIMB THE HILL, WAITING WON'T SHRINK IT.

A FAST HORSE CANNOT GO FAST FAR.

THE MORE YOU'VE GOT,

THE MORE WHAT YOU'VE GOT HAS GOT YOU.

If you have
nothing to do,
don't do it.

THERE ARE NO FRIENDLY RATTLERS.

Good grazing makes those who
are there happy, and attracts
those who are far off.

THOSE WHO KNOW DON'T
TALK. THOSE WHO TALK
DON'T KNOW.
THOSE WHO MOO DO.

Swatting flies is a thankless job,

but nonetheless important.

When the soul lies down in fresh, sweet
grass, the world is too full to talk about.

THE EASIEST RELATIONSHIP IS
TO BE A PART OF THE HERD.
THE HARDEST IS TO BE APART
FROM IT.

It's easy to be content with your lot if it's a feed lot.

ANYONE CONCERNED ABOUT
THEIR DIGNITY SHOULD
MAKE A POINT NEVER TO
RIDE A BULL.

TOO MUCH
AIN'T HEALTHY.

IT'S NOT THE SHARPEST SPURS THAT DO THE MOST DAMAGE.

JUST BEING HAS NOT
BEEN GIVEN ITS DUE.
STOP THINKING SO MUCH;
CHEW YOUR CUD A WHILE.

Each day is a link in a mighty long chain.

IT'S BETTER TO TELL THE
TRUTH AND RUN THAN TO
LIE AND GET CAUGHT.

NOTHING IS SO ORDINARY AS WANTING TO BE REMARKABLE.

The only way to
a clean stable

is to get dirty.

YOU CAN'T
SHOE A RUNNING
HORSE.

- "FORKED DOWN" IS LANDING ON YOUR HEAD WITH YOUR RUSTY DUSTY UP IN THE AIR.

- **"FORK END UP" IS LANDING ON YOUR SIT-DOWN WITH YOUR LEGS UP IN THE AIR.**

- JUST PLAIN "FORKED" MEANS IT'S OVER—THERE'S NOTHING UP IN THE AIR.

You can't convince a rooster he doesn't know as much about singin' as a mockingbird.

WHAT'S A
METAPHOR?

A place for cows to graze in.

YOU CAN COVER IT WITH SUGAR
AND BAKE IT IN THE OVEN, BUT A
COW PIE IS STILL MANURE.

Never do anything
you can't moo about
after dinner.

IF YOU STRADDLE THE FENCE,

★ ★ ★

YOU'LL NEVER HAVE YOUR FEET ON THE GROUND.

THE ONLY WAY BETWEEN
A ROCK AND A HARD
PLACE IS THROUGH IT.

DRINK NOT THE MILK OF AMNESIA.

Finding a worm in your apple
is a lot better than finding half
a worm in your apple.

"There's something in the way she moos."

When given a
choice, a critter
will always head
for the wrong gate.

DON'T DO NOTHIN' TOO MUCH.

They made
tomorrow so you
wouldn't have to eat
everything today.

IF YOU WAIT
BY THE GATE,

IT WILL OPEN.

The water won't
clear up until
you get the hogs
outta the creek.

SOME SHOO FLIES.

OTHERS LET THEM GO BAREFOOT.

A STAMPEDE
HAS NO
CONSCIENCE.

SHORT STIRRUPS MAKE FOR A BAD RIDE.

The path
continuously followed

becomes a habit.

THE MORE PROMISES YOU MAKE TODAY, THE MORE EXCUSES YOU MAKE TOMORROW.

THE SUN DOES NOT RISE TO HEAR THE ROOSTER CROW.

A NIGHT OF SOWING WILD OATS

MAKES FOR A POOR BREAKFAST.

If you've ever wondered what horse feed tastes like, eat a handful of unsalted baked tortilla chips.

WHEN THE HORSE DIES, IT WILL DO NO GOOD TO:

- CHANGE RIDERS.
- MOVE THE BODY TO A NEW LOCATION.
- GET A SHARPER PAIR OF SPURS.
- SAY, "IT'LL BE ALL RIGHT. WE'VE ALWAYS RIDDEN HORSES LIKE THIS ONE."

- COMPLAIN ABOUT THE STATE OF HORSES THESE DAYS.
- TIGHTEN THE CINCH.
- BLAME THE HORSE'S PARENTS.
- HAVE A COMMITTEE WORK OUT A PLAN TO GET THE HORSE BACK ON ITS FEET.

Never spur a horse
when he's swimmin'.

IF YOU THROW YOUR LOOP HALF
A DOZEN TIMES AND MISS YOUR
MARK, THE ONLY THING TO DO IS
LIE ABOUT IT.

IF IT'S YOUR
BEHIND THAT'S
ITCHIN',
★ ★ ★
IT WON'T DO ANY
GOOD TO SCRATCH
YOUR HEAD.

A COMFORTABLE RIDE IS WHAT'S BEST FOR PONY AND RIDER.

A wild horse has
more secrets than
a gentle one.

It's easier
to catch a
horse than
to ride one.

TAKE LIFE WITH A LICK OF SALT.

IF YOU STICK YOUR HEAD IN THE SAND,

YOU CAN EXPECT A KICK IN THE TAIL.

THE SMILE AND THE RAINBOW WHISPER HOPE.

Many are cold, but some are frozen.

THE BIG DIFFERENCE BETWEEN
ANIMALS AND HUMANS IS THAT
ANIMALS HAVE A HEALTHIER
SEX LIFE.

First came man, then woman, or something like that. Either way, if they wanted to ride, they needed a horse, so then came the horse.

IF YOU LOOK A
GIFT HORSE IN
THE MOUTH,
YOU COULD
LOSE A NOSE.

LIFE IS RELATIVE.

IF A RACCOON PICKS A LOCK, HE GETS FEATURED ON NATURE. IF A MAN DOES IT, HE GETS THREE TO FIVE IN THE HOOSEGOW.

The smoother the gab, the smoother the dose.

You don't know you've been had 'til you've swallowed it.

A horse by any other name would still be a horse. Same goes for a jackass.

A BLIND HORSE SEES JUST AS WELL FROM EITHER END.